RAFFI
EVERGREEN EVERBLUE

Amsco Publications
New York • London • Sydney

DESIGN CONCEPT AND ART BY RAFFI AND FRED/ALAN INC.
PHOTOGRAPHY BY DAVIES AND STARR

THIS BOOK COPYRIGHT © 1992 BY HOMELAND PUBLISHING (SOCAN),
A DIVISION OF TROUBADOUR RECORDS LTD.
PUBLISHED BY AMSCO PUBLICATIONS,
A DIVISION OF MUSIC SALES CORPORATION, NEW YORK
ALL RIGHTS RESERVED

ORDER NO. AM 90036
US INTERNATIONAL STANDARD BOOK NUMBER: 0.8256.1340.X
UK INTERNATIONAL STANDARD BOOK NUMBER: 0.7119.3112.7

EXCLUSIVE DISTRIBUTORS:
MUSIC SALES CORPORATION
225 PARK AVENUE SOUTH, NEW YORK, NEW YORK 10003 USA
MUSIC SALES LIMITED
8/9 FRITH STREET, LONDON W1P 3LA ENGLAND
MUSIC SALES PTY LIMITED
120 ROTHSCHILD STREET, ROSEBERY, SYDNEY NSW 2018 AUSTRALIA

PRINTED AND BOUND IN THE UNITED STATES OF AMERICA
BY VICKS LITHOGRAPH AND PRINTING CORPORATION

Evergreen Everblue 4

Mama's Kitchen 15

Big Beautiful Planet 10

Alive and Dreaming 20

Where I Live 24

What's The Matter With Us 28

Our Dear, Dear Mother 33

Just Like The Sun 38

Clean Rain 41

One Light, One Sun 52

We Are Not Alone 46

Evergreen Everblue

Words and Music by Raffi

Copyright © 1990 Homeland Publishing (SOCAN), a division of Troubadour Records Ltd.
International Copyright Secured. All Rights Reserved. Used by Permission.

Big Beautiful Planet

Words and Music by Raffi

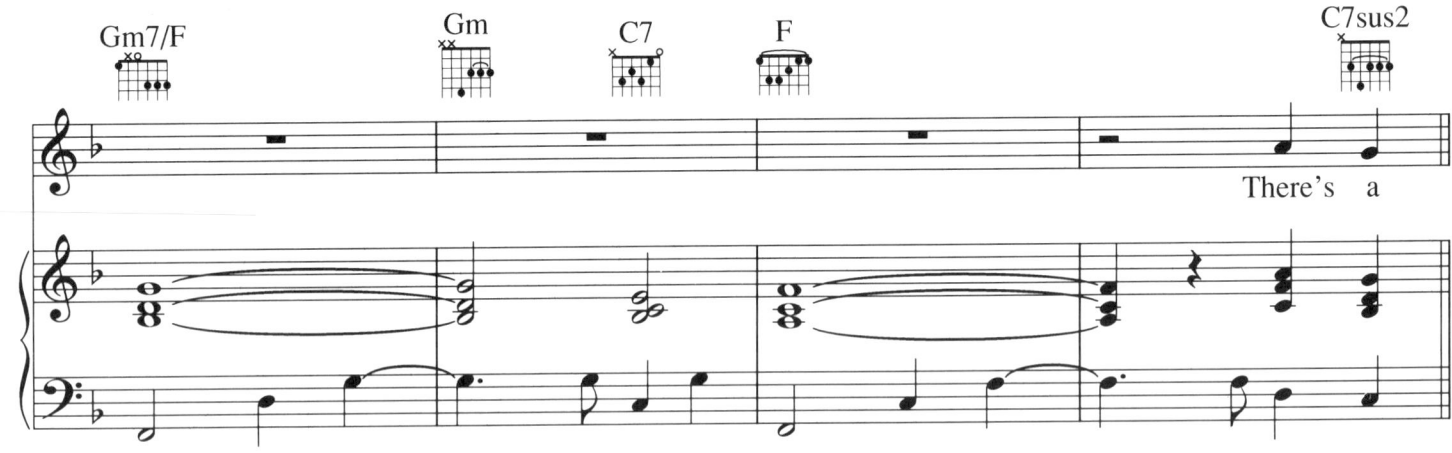

Copyright © 1982 Homeland Publishing (SOCAN), a division of Troubadour Records Ltd.
International Copyright Secured. All Rights Reserved. Used by Permission.

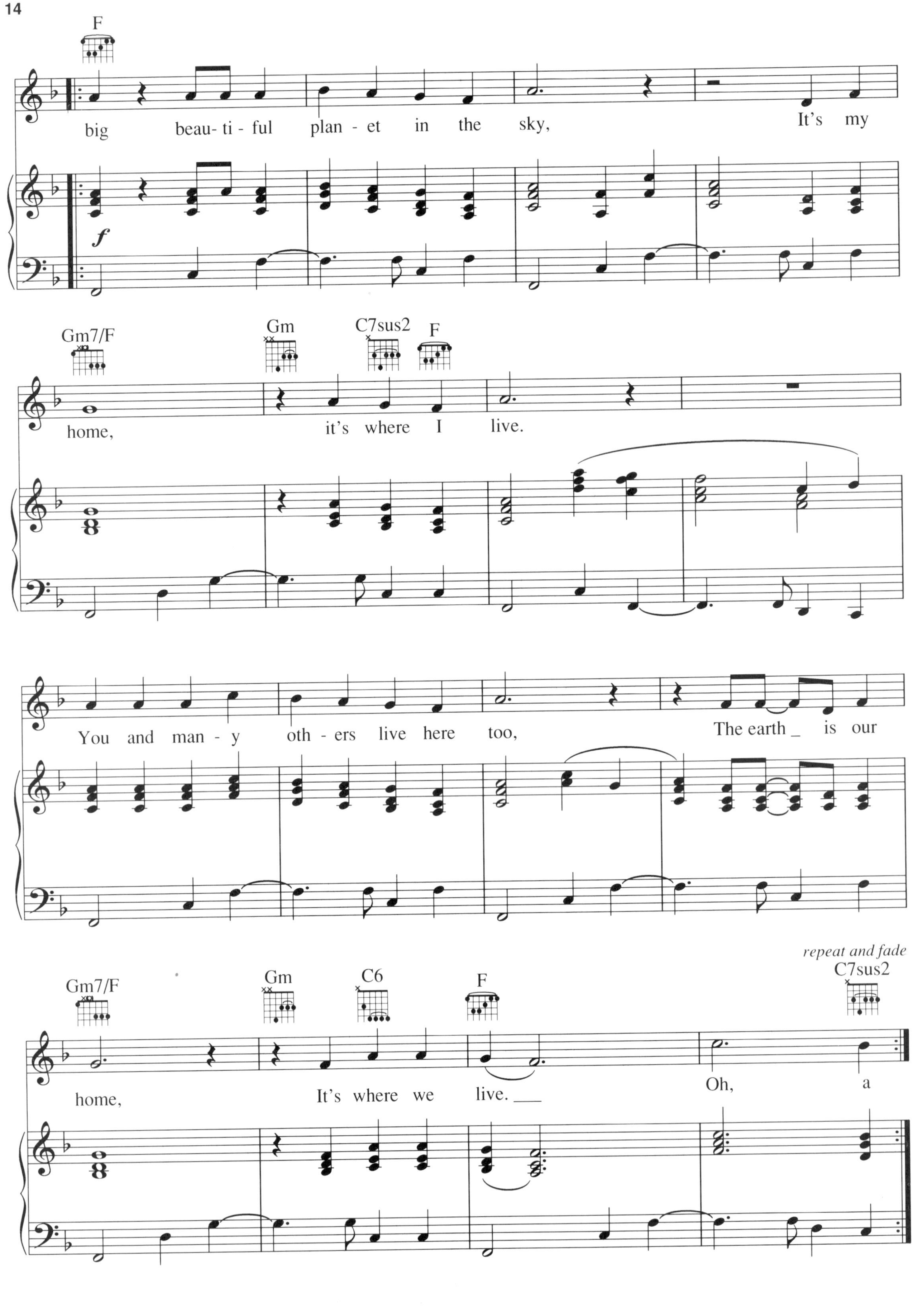
F
big beau-ti-ful plan-et in the sky, It's my
f
Gm7/F
Gm
C7sus2
F
home, it's where I live.
You and man-y oth-ers live here too, The earth _ is our
Gm7/F
Gm
C6
F
home, It's where we live. ___
repeat and fade
C7sus2
Oh, a

Mama's Kitchen

Words and Music by Raffi

Ma-ma's kitch-en got no dress code, you just come and eat your fill, yeah, yeah, yeah, yeah.

Copyright © 1990 Homeland Publishing (SOCAN), a division of Troubadour Records Ltd.
International Copyright Secured. All Rights Reserved. Used by Permission.

Alive and Dreaming

Words and Music by Raffi

Copyright © 1990 Homeland Publishing (SOCAN), a division of Troubadour Records Ltd.
International Copyright Secured. All Rights Reserved. Used by Permission.

Where I Live

Words and Music by Raffi

Copyright © 1990 Homeland Publishing (SOCAN), a division of Troubadour Records Ltd.
International Copyright Secured. All Rights Reserved. Used by Permission.

What's The Matter With Us

Words and Music by Raffi

So many countries to know. Why so afraid of living when there's so much lovin' to do. What's the matter with us? I'm asking do you know what's the matter with us? Ah. (Optional: Day day lay da-dn-du day, la-du-da-nt da da da da da da.) What's the

Repeat under Rap, then fade.

Rap lyrics

What's the matter? We out of control.
    Some are giving up, and even lost their souls.
Killing each other for a little piece of gold,
    And why, homeboy? I don't know.
Some are giving up on mankind,
    Saying that true love is hard to find.
What's the matter? Huh, I ask myself.
    I put the mankind's thoughts and pack them on the shelf.
What's the matter? Tell me please.
    I'm asking God. Yeah, I'm down on my knees.
I'm trying to figure out why I've given up trying.
    What's the matter, homeboy? Can you tell me why?
Don't raise a fuss—
    We need to get together, all of us.
Huh, we giving up.
    As someone say: that what we're coming to.
Yeah, I telling you, homeboy,
    We can't give it up, no way.
You tell me, homeboy, so much has gone to waste,
    Reeking of disposable. Mad situation all over the place.
You know what I mean—
    It ain't the same; it's a different kind of scene.
We lost our minds.
    Someone's giving up on mankind!

Our Dear, Dear Mother

Words and Music by Raffi

way. But now we're look-in' to you to feel our way home. Yes, and with hope in our hearts, we're com-in' back home, home to you. Our dear, dear

D.S. al Fine

Just Like The Sun

Words and Music by Raffi

Moderately slow

1. Just like the birds that keep on fly-ing, Just like the wind that keeps on blow-ing, I see a wave of o-ceans roll-ing

---

Copyright © 1987 Homeland Publishing (SOCAN), a division of Troubadour Records Ltd.
International Copyright Secured. All Rights Reserved. Used by Permission.

A D D/F♯ Bm E E7
on and on, Just like the sun, these gifts are here for
A Asus4 A D A Asus4 A
ev - ery - one. 2. Just like the trees that keep on giv - ing, Just like the
D A Asus4 A D E
grass that keeps on grow - ing, I hear the sound of chil - dren sing - ing
A D D/F♯ 1. Bm E
on and on Just like the sun, these gifts are here for

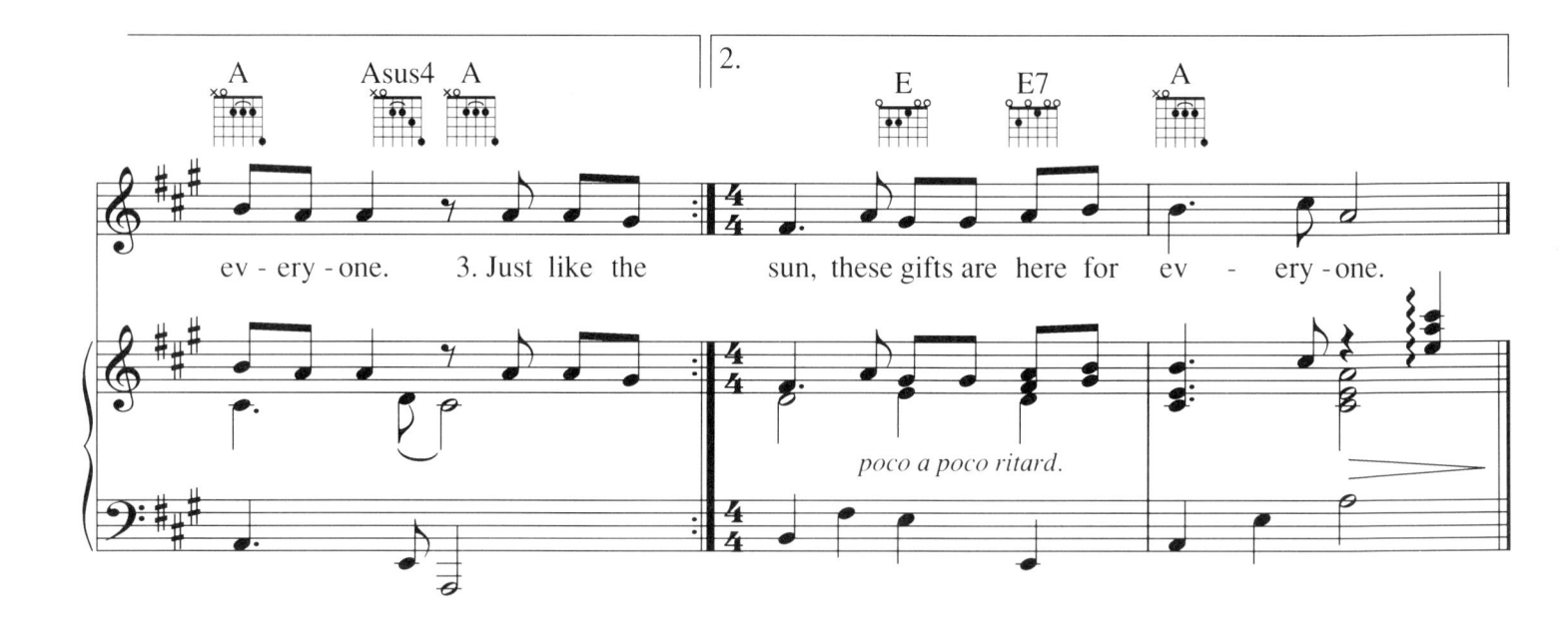

Additional lyrics

3. Just as the flowers keep on blooming,
   Just like the leaves that keep on turning (for us),
   I feel the change of seasons flowing on and on,
   Just like the sun, these gifts are here for everyone.

4. Just like the moon that keeps on shining,
   Just like the stars that keep on twinkling,
   I know a world of wonders playing on and on,
   Just like the sun, these gifts are here for everyone.

Clean Rain

Words and Music by Raffi

Brightly

(optional duet)

Clean _____ rain, crys-tal clean rain, Sing-ing

Copyright © 1990 Homeland Publishing (SOCAN), a division of Troubadour Records Ltd.
International Copyright Secured. All Rights Reserved. Used by Permission.

clean _____ rain. Oh, I re-mem-ber the days when the rain fell clean In-to the val-leys and in-to the streams. Clean through the air and clean to the earth, They say that the rain fell clean.

Rain on the land and rain in the wa-ter,

Clean fell the rain from the skies a-bove. The

rain brought life, life in ev-ery drop, The

rain that we used to know.

There's life in the woods and life in our waters, Moving in the beauty of this earth that we love, And praying for the day when the

B7 B7/F♯ Em C
rain falls clean, Like the rain we
D7 G Gsus4 G
used to know.
G Em C D7
Clean rain, crys - tal clean rain, sing - ing
f
G Em C D
repeat and fade
clean rain.

We Are Not Alone

Words and Music by Raffi

Moderately, steady

We are not a - lone, _____ those of us who care that the com-ing gen-e-ra-tions might live free from con-ta-mi-na-tion.

Copyright © 1990 Homeland Publishing (SOCAN), a division of Troubadour Records Ltd.
International Copyright Secured. All Rights Reserved. Used by Permission.

47

We are not a-lone__ some-thing tells me, we are not a-lone. And we are not a-fraid___ to make our feel-ings known,___ To help our friends and neigh-bors to share in our con-cern. Won't you lis-ten with your heart to this song of ours: We are not a-lone.

48

We're cry-ing, "Shut down the spread of a-tom-ic waste." We're cry-ing, "Shut down the threat of a nuc-le-ar haze!" We're say-ing, "No more can we be-lieve that it's safe To hide our heads in the sand, And pre-tend not to un-der-stand The poi - son -ing ____ of our land." Oh,

Coda

not a - lone. (We are not a - lone. ____) For the sake of our

chil - dren, let us come to our sens - es. In the name of

love, let us come to our sens - es. In the threat to

life, no-bod-y pro-fits. There is-n't a mo-ment to lose ___ while we still have a chance to choose where our fu-ture goes. Oh, We are not a-lone, ___ those of us who care that the com-ing gen-e-ra-tions might live free from con-ta-mi-na-tion. We are not a-lone, some-thing tells me we are not a-lone. (We are not a-lone.) Oh, we are not a-lone. (We are not a-lone.) We are not a-lone.

melody

repeat and fade

(We are not a-lone.) We are

One Light, One Sun

Words and Music by Raffi

1. One light, one sun. One sun lighting ev'ry- one. One world turning. One world turning.
2. One world, one home. One world home for ev'ry- one. One dream, one song.

Copyright © 1985 Homeland Publishing (SOCAN), a division of Troubadour Records Ltd.
International Copyright Secured. All Rights Reserved. Used by Permission.

1. One world turn-ing ev-'ry-one.

2. One song heard by ev-'ry-one.

3. One love, one heart. One heart warm-ing ev-'ry-one. One hope, one joy.

One love fill-ing ev-'ry-one. Oh, _____

4. One light, one sun. ___ One sun light-ing ev-'ry-one. One light warm-ing ev-'ry-one.

Da da da da da da.

ritard. e dim.

EVERGREEN EVER BLUE